To: _____

From: _____

Published by C.R. Gibson® Norwalk, CT 06856
C.R. Gibson® is a registered trademark of Thomas Nelson, Inc.
Made in the U.S.A.
ISBN 0-7667-1731-3
GB650

Listen To Your Angel

photographs by
Kim Anderson

text by Julie Mitchell Marra

THE C.R. GIBSON COMPANY NORWALK, CONNECTICUT

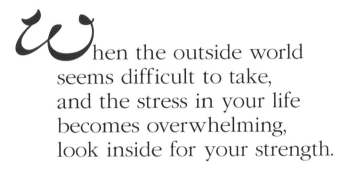

When the outside world
seems difficult to take,
and the stress in your life
becomes overwhelming,
look inside for your strength.

Take some quiet time to meditate on where you have been, and where you want to go.

You will find the power to create change within yourself.

You are a unique creation...

able to achieve all the goals
that you set your mind and heart on.

Your courage and enthusiasm
will see you through to victory!

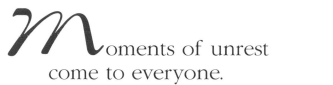oments of unrest
come to everyone.
But peace comes after the storm,
and then you will begin to see
with fresh eyes all that you
have been given.

*W*hen you encounter doubt,
disagreements or impediments,
don't let discouragement lead you astray.
Focus on your purpose,
and head toward your goal.

*W*hen faced with obstacles
that seem overwhelming,

open your eyes, look for a new road
and head in a new direction.
You might find a wonderful surprise
waiting for you, just around the bend.

*Y*ou have the power to make your world a better place.

You create your own attitude.
If your thoughts are positive,
then your world will be, too.

*The time will come
for you to make decisions.*

Think each one through.
Rely on your instincts and
trust your heart.

*S*ing your song with confidence.
You have a beautiful
melody inside you.
Share it with the world!

*S*ing the song of success...
explore your options...
experience each moment...
believe in yourself!

Some days patience will be all you need...

if you see your dream
but can't seem to get close enough
to touch it,
be patient and know that if you keep
reaching for the stars,
They will be yours very soon.

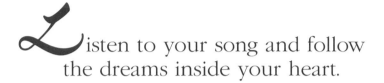

*L*isten to your song and follow
the dreams inside your heart.

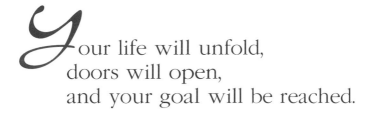

$\mathcal{Y}$our life will unfold,
doors will open,
and your goal will be reached.

Listen to your angel.

Other Kim Anderson Gift Books:

Babies Are a Special Gift
For My Friend
Our Lives Were Meant to be Shared
To My Sister
Thank You for Being You

Colophon
Editor: Eileen D'Andrea
Design: Elizabeth Woll

Type set in Charme,
Garamond Light and Garamond Bold